EXPLORING INDIA WITH CORDELIA CRUISES

First edition. June 11, 2024.

ISBN: 979-8227559340

Written by Prabhakar Veeraraghavan.

Table of Contents

Exploring India with Cordelia Cruises

By : Prabhakar Veeraraghavan

Exploring India with Cordelia Cruises

———◦◦———

Voyages of Elegance
By : Prabhakar Veeraraghavan

———◦◦———

**Copyright © 2024
by Prabhakar Veeraraghavan
All rights reserved.**

Type of book

The book "**Travel by Cordelia Cruises in India**" is primarily a travel guide. This type of book typically serves the following purposes: **Travelogue** : **Narrative:** It often includes personal anecdotes and stories from the author's experiences, providing readers with an engaging and immersive narrative.

Exploration: It explores various destinations along the cruise routes, giving insights into the culture, history, and attractions of each port of call. Guidebook: Practical Information: It offers practical information about cruising with Cordelia Cruises, such as booking details, room selection, dining options, onboard activities, and excursions.

Recommendations: It provides recommendations on must-see sights, activities, and dining options at different ports.

Lifestyle and Leisure: Luxurious Experiences: It highlights the luxurious aspects of cruising with Cordelia Cruises, focusing on amenities, entertainment, and unique experiences offered onboard.

Wellness and Relaxation: It may include sections on spa treatments, wellness programs, and relaxation techniques available during the cruise. Cultural Insight: Cultural Exploration: It delves into the cultural and historical significance of the destinations visited, enriching the reader's understanding of the places and people encountered.

Local Cuisine: It explores local culinary delights available both onboard and at various ports, providing a gastronomic journey.

About the author

PRABHAKAR VEERARAGHAVAN is a Blogger and an accomplished KDP Author after spending more than 2 decades in the corporate world. He is passionate in writing books with an innate ability to transport readers to captivating words and evoke profound emotions.

Combining remarkable creativity with meticulous attention to detail, my idea is to intricate plots that leave readers spellbound from the first page to the last. The motive is not to leave the reads just for the sake of reading but to involve them deep into the subject that have mind blowing effect upon completion of every book.

Section 1 : What is a Cruise?

A cruise is a voyage on a large passenger ship that offers a leisure travel experience on water, typically including stops at various ports along the route. Cruises are known for providing an all-inclusive vacation experience, where the price often includes accommodations, meals, entertainment, and various onboard activities.

Key Features of a Cruise:

1. **Accommodations**:
Passengers stay in cabins or staterooms, which can range from basic interior rooms to luxurious suites with balconies.

Modern cruises often feature a variety of room types to suit different budgets and preferences.

2. **Dining**:
Cruises offer a wide range of dining options, including formal dining rooms, casual buffets, specialty restaurants, and room service.

Many cruises provide all-inclusive meal plans, allowing passengers to enjoy diverse culinary experiences.

3. **Entertainment and Activities**:
Cruises are equipped with a plethora of entertainment options such as theatres, live music, dance performances, comedy shows, and movie screenings.

Onboard activities can include swimming pools, water slides, sports courts, gyms, spas, and casinos.

Some cruises offer educational lectures, cooking classes, and themed events.

4. **Sore Excursions:**

Cruises typically stop at various ports, allowing passengers to disembark and explore different destinations.

Shore excursions can include guided tours, cultural experiences, beach outings, shopping trips, and adventure activities.

5. **Itineraries:**

Cruises offer a variety of itineraries, ranging from short weekend trips to extended voyages lasting several weeks.

Popular cruise routes include the Caribbean, Mediterranean, Alaska, and river cruises through Europe and Asia.

6. **All-Inclusive Experience:**

Many cruises provide an all-inclusive package, covering most of the expenses, which makes it easier for passengers to manage their travel budget.

Additional services such as specialty dining, spa treatments, and shore excursions may incur extra costs.

Benefits of Cruising:

Convenience : Cruises provide a hassle-free travel experience as accommodations, meals, and entertainment are all located in one place.

Variety: Passengers can visit multiple destinations without the need to unpack and repack or arrange transportation between locations.

Social Experience: Cruises offer a social environment where passengers can meet and interact with fellow travellers.

Family-Friendly: Many cruises offer facilities and activities tailored for children and families, making them a popular choice for family vacations.

Examples of Cruise Lines:

Royal Caribbean International : Known for its large ships and innovative amenities.

Carnival Cruise Line: Popular for its fun and affordable cruises.

Norwegian Cruise Line: Offers a flexible "freestyle cruising" experience.

Disney Cruise Line: Specializes in family-oriented cruises with Disney-themed entertainment.

Cruise Travel in India

India offers a variety of exciting cruise options that showcase its beautiful coastline, rich culture, and stunning landscapes. Here are some popular cruises in India:

1. Cordelia Cruises

Cordelia Cruises is a prominent player in the Indian cruise industry, offering luxurious and memorable cruising experiences. They provide several itineraries including:

Mumbai to Goa

Mumbai to Diu

Mumbai to Lakshadweep

Chennai to Maldives

Chennai to Galle

Chennai to Trincomalee

Chennai Visakhapatnam Puducherry and Chennai.

Cordelia Cruises focus on providing a blend of modern amenities and traditional Indian hospitality, making them a popular choice for travellers.

2. The Angriya Cruise

Angriya Cruise operates between Mumbai and Goa, providing a luxurious and scenic voyage along the Konkan coast. Key features include:

Route: Mumbai to Goa

Duration: Overnight cruise

Highlights: Infinity pool, multiple dining options, bars, and a spa.

3. Lakshadweep Cruises

Lakshadweep Cruises offer an opportunity to explore the pristine islands of Lakshadweep. These cruises typically depart from Kochi and cover several islands in the archipelago.

Route: Kochi to Lakshadweep

Duration: Various options ranging from 5 to 7 days

Highlights: Water sports, scuba diving, snorkelling, and exploring the unique marine life.

4. Sundarbans Luxury Cruise

This cruise takes you through the Sundarbans, the world's largest mangrove forest and home to the Bengal tiger.

Route: Kolkata to Sundarbans

Duration: 3 to 4 days

Highlights: Wildlife safaris, village tours, and bird watching.

5. Brahmaputra River Cruise

Explore the northeastern part of India with a cruise on the Brahmaputra River, offering a unique perspective on Assam's culture and natural beauty.

Route: Various routes on the Brahmaputra River, often starting from Guwahati

Duration: 7 to 10 days

Highlights: Wildlife, tea garden visits, cultural performances, and visits to ancient temples.

6. M.V. Mahabaahu Cruise

A luxury cruise on the Brahmaputra River, M.V. Mahabaahu offers an immersive experience in Assam.

Route: Guwahati to Jorhat (or reverse)

Duration: 7 days

Highlights: Kaziranga National Park visit, tea estate tour, traditional dance performances, and exploring Majuli Island.

7. Goa Cruises

Several short cruises operate along the coast of Goa, offering scenic views and a relaxed atmosphere.

Types: Sunset cruises, dinner cruises, backwater cruises

Duration: Few hours to full-day excursions

Highlights: Scenic views of the Goan coastline, traditional Goan cuisine, live music, and dance performances.

These cruises provide diverse experiences, from luxurious ocean voyages to intimate river cruises, catering to a wide range of preferences and interests.

[Cordelia Cruises](https://www.cordeliacruises.com/)

[Angriya Cruises](https://www.angriyacruises.com/)

[Lakshadweep Cruises](https://www.lakshadweeptourism.com/)

[Sunderbans   Luxury
Cruise](https://www.sunderbansluxurycruise.com/)
   [Brahmaputra   River
Cruises](https://www.assambengalnavigation.com/)
   [M.V. Mahabaahu](https://www.mvmahabaahu.com/)
   [Goa Cruises](https://www.goatourism.gov.in/)

Exploring these options can help you find the perfect cruise to experience the beauty and diversity of India.

Cordelia Cruises India

Cordelia Cruises is a prominent cruise company in India, having recently acquired ships from Royal Caribbean International, including the renowned Empress of the Seas in late December 2020. This acquisition introduces a new era of luxury cruising to the Indian Ocean.

Cordelia Cruises aims to promote a blend of modern and traditional cruise culture, offering Indians an exceptional holiday experience. The luxury ship promises to redefine vacationing, providing a range of opulent amenities and services.

Onboard, guests will enjoy exceptional hospitality services, designed to make them feel at home. The cruise delivers international standards of service, ensuring a memorable journey even while in their home country.

A Journey of Empress Of The Seas

Take a quick tour of the Empress of the Seas, now proudly owned by Cordelia Cruises, a renowned organization in India. This magnificent cruise ship is nothing short of a dream come true, captivating everyone with its stunning beauty and charm.

Onboard, you will experience unparalleled enthusiasm and elegance. The Empress of the Seas offers limitless excitement with gourmet meals, engaging activities, and live concerts, ensuring a memorable voyage.

The cruise serves India's premier ports, including Chennai, Kochi, Mumbai, Visakhapatnam, Mormugao, and Lakshadweep, as well as international destinations like Sri Lanka. Based on video footage and photos, the ship prominently features a large "Cordelia Cruises" logo on its hull, symbolizing its new journey in the Indian Ocean.

The Empress promises unforgettable memories, from breathtaking sunsets to stunning sunrises. Originally launched by Admiral Cruises and later operated by Royal Caribbean International, the ship debuted in 1990 as Nordic Express before being renamed Empress of the Seas.

Having sailed routes in San Juan, the Bahamas, Puerto Rico, Bermuda, and South America, the Empress is now set to explore the Indian East and West ports under Cordelia Cruises, operated by Waterways Tourism Pvt Ltd. This transition marks a new chapter in its illustrious history, bringing world-class cruising experiences to Indian waters.

Section 2 : Everything You want to know about the Seas :

Here are the minute details you need to know about the cruise before boarding it. Please go through every section given below.

Technical Details of the Ship

◈ Type: Empress-class cruise ship
◈ Capacity: 1,840
◈ Crew: 668
◈ Cabins: 796 Cabins
◈ Speed: 19.5 knots (36.1 km/h; 22.4 mph)
◈ Draught: 7.10 m (23.29 ft)
◈ Decks: 11 Passenger Decks
◈ Installed power: 2 × Wärtsilä-Duvant Crespelle diesel combined 16,200 kW
◈ Tonnage: 48,563 GT / 5,344 DWT
◈ Length: 210.81 m (691.63 ft)
◈ Beam: 30.70 m (100.72 ft)

A Journey of Empress of the Seas

Let's take a quick tour of the Empress of the Seas, now proudly owned by Cordelia Cruises, a distinguished organization in India. This stunning cruise ship is a dream come true, captivating everyone with its beauty and charm.

Onboard, you'll be immersed in an atmosphere of enthusiasm and elegance. The Empress of the Seas offers unlimited thrills with gourmet meals, exciting activities, and live concerts, ensuring an unforgettable experience.

The cruise serves several of India's premier ports, including Chennai, Kochi, Mumbai, Visakhapatnam, Mormugao, and Lakshadweep, as well as international destinations like Sri Lanka. The ship features a prominent "Cordelia Cruises" logo on its hull, symbolizing its new journey across the Indian Ocean.

The Empress promises to create lasting memories, from breathtaking sunsets to stunning sunrises. Originally launched by Admiral Cruises and later operated by Royal Caribbean International, the ship debuted in 1990 as Nordic Express before being renamed Empress of the Seas.

Having sailed through San Juan, the Bahamas, Puerto Rico, Bermuda, and South America, the Empress is now set to explore the Indian East and West ports under Cordelia Cruises, managed by Waterways Tourism Pvt Ltd. This transition marks a new chapter in its illustrious history, bringing world-class cruising experiences to Indian waters.

What will you get when you are onboard?

Well, you can wake up in the middle of the ocean and enjoy its freshness and rhythmic music. No doubt, Empress of the seas is the most luxurious cruise in India. You will be astonished by its onboard accommodations, delicious food, and a refreshing experience.

Why is Empress of the Seas best among other cruises?

We knew that you would have this question. Here is the solution for why Cordelia Cruise's Empress of the Seas is the best among another huge cruise: –

- ◈ Excellent Food – 3 Special Restaurants
- ◈ Indian & International cuisines
- ◈ 5 Bars and various party zones
- ◈ Fitness Centre
- ◈ Spa & Salon
- ◈ Casino in international waters
- ◈ Live Bands and DJ Parties
- ◈ Adventure activities
- ◈ Theatre
- ◈ Swimming Pool
- ◈ Nightclub and Lounges

◈ Luxury cruise experience

◈ Non-stop Entertainment

◈ Shopping

◈ Discos and Party Places

◈ Broadway-themed halls with world-class musicians, comedians, and dancers

1) Inclusive Services

◈ **Variety of Food:** Empress offers various dining options onboard, such as Continental, oriental, Mughlai, and even Indian street food. You will enjoy Southeast Asia's taste onboard with our oriental restaurant calling attention from Japan's flavors to Thailand. Either, you can enjoy the elegant dishes made by our talented chefs. Even if you want some quick plates, we have a food plaza for you, where you will have pizzas, tandoors, grills, and Indian street food. Moreover, we have a special place for Jain food to make you feel delightful while maintaining your diet.

◈ **Homeliness:** Housing for you that will make you feel homely and luxurious.

◈ **Sun- Soaked Pool Fun:** Nothing can be greater than starting the day diving into the pool. Pool time, not only cheer up kids, but the adults also love it. So, spend your time at the pool area, along with your kids.

◈ **Adventurous Activities:** Adventure on the ship! Sounds great. You will explore rock-climbing wall facilities onboard for thrill lovers with many compelling activities.

◇ **Casinos:** Casinos will be open for everyone, free of cost.

◇ **The Party Place:** Can't imagine the thrill of the party in the middle of the ocean? Then, experience it with us. We have The Dome for you to make your trip unforgettable.

◇ **Food that your child will love to have:** It's so boring to have the usual food on a tour. Isn't it? Thus, the cruise company has hired skillful chefs for you to take care of your desires by cooking international cuisines. Family dining is definitely an inevitable culture of India; therefore, the staff looks after every minor aspect.

◇ **Exclusive Reading Zone:** A long journey along with a quiet and calm environment is the perfect scenery to read books. Cruise has special reading zones for the book lovers at Empress, which has an inspiring books collection.

◇ **Fitness spot:** You'll have access to the gym and fitness centres.

◇ **Entertainment:** Entertainment facilities, in the form of live music shows and stand-up comedy.

2) Exclusive services

◇ A place with a seating capacity of 740 guests is made. You will experience the glamor and fashion of beauty shows onboard by world-class performers.

◇ Glow while on holiday with our Spa and Salon service. Being on holiday, you need to be more pampered. So, we have arrangements for you to glow with our spa therapist and salon services. You can also book an appointment with them, for the wedding or other occasions.

◇ If you wish to watch the additional entertainment shows from our performer artist, you will have to book the show.

◇ Shopping! No matter where we are, shopping makes us happy. Steal a little time from your cruise holiday, and visit the shopping centre onboard.

ONBOARDING PRICE ON Cordelia Cruises

If you were eagerly waiting for a fun family holiday, this is the best time for it. Surprise your family with a holiday plan like never before. Take them to a new world of amusement on the cruise.

We assure you that these bunches of amazing provisions by Cordelia cruise will be one of your most comfortable journeys. Wait, are you pondering upon the Cordelia Cruise prices?

Well, you are thinking in the right place. However, luxury is not so cheap. But, you will be happy to know that the price for the tour will not put so much of a burden on your pocket. The Empress is offering so many facilities to you, for which the fare, for your tour, is justifying. Also, the price depends on your boarding and destination point, which may differ.

So, if you are also willing to spend some quality time with your family and loved ones and want them to enjoy leaving the pandemic situation behind, do book the tour. This journey will be unforgettable for you and your family.

Section 3 : Cordelia Cruise | Chennai - Visakhapatnam - Puducherry – Chennai.

Cordelia Cruises: Chennai - Visakhapatnam - Puducherry - Chennai (6 Days & 5 Nights)

Meeting Location: Island Grounds, Flag Staff Road, Port Trust Officers Quarters, Sathya Nagar, Chennai Port Trust, Chennai, Tamilnadu, 60009.

Departure Dates(2024): 3 June, 17 June, 1 July, 15 July, 29 July, 12 Aug, 26 Aug, 9 Sep

Check-in/Departure:

⬦ 8:30 PM (3 June)
⬦ 6:00 PM (23 September)

Note: Please reach the meeting location one hour before departure.
Check-Out/Arrival:

⬦ 9:00 AM (5 June)
⬦ 8:00 AM (25 September)

About the Cruise

Embark on an unforgettable cruising adventure from Chennai, gliding through the azure waters of the Bay of Bengal. Experience the sheer bliss of endless ocean views that will rejuvenate your spirit. Spend two luxurious nights aboard the magnificent Cordelia Cruise, staying in the plush rooms of The Empress. Enjoy a memorable getaway with your loved ones, indulging in various opulent amenities. Relish a variety of delectable Indian and international cuisines throughout your journey. Immerse yourself in the lively entertainment programs, or unwind with a soothing spa session. This cruise promises a perfect blend of relaxation, luxury, and fun.

Experience an extraordinary 6-day, 5-night voyage with Cordelia Cruises, sailing from Chennai to Visakhapatnam, Puducherry, and back to Chennai. Enjoy the breathtaking panoramic views of the ocean, filling your soul with pure bliss as you cruise across the stunning Bay of Bengal.

Stay in your choice of accommodations, including Suite, Mini-Suite, Ocean View, and Interior rooms, ensuring a comfortable and luxurious stay. Delight in a variety of delectable Indian and international cuisines throughout your journey. Dance to lively entertainment programs or unwind with a relaxing spa session. This magnificent cruise offers the perfect blend of adventure, luxury, and relaxation.

Embark on an exhilarating 6-day, 5-night cruise with Cordelia Cruises, exploring the serene Bay of Bengal and visiting vibrant coastal cities. Here are the highlights and details of this remarkable voyage:

Itinerary:

1. Day 1: Chennai Departure
Board the cruise in Chennai and set sail towards Visakhapatnam. Settle into your elegantly designed room and explore the ship's numerous amenities.

2. Day 2: At Sea
Spend the day at sea enjoying various onboard activities such as spa treatments, gym sessions, and entertainment shows. Try your luck at the casino or relax by the pool.

3. Day 3: Visakhapatnam
Arrive in Visakhapatnam. Explore the city's attractions, such as its beautiful beaches and historical sites. Return to the ship for a night of entertainment and dining.

4. Day 4: At Sea
Enjoy another day on the high seas with a range of activities, including live music, dance shows, and various onboard games and workshops.

5. Day 5: Puducherry
Dock at Puducherry and spend the day exploring its French colonial architecture, vibrant markets, and serene beaches. Head back to the ship for an evening of fun and relaxation.

6. Day 6: Return to Chennai
Arrive back in Chennai in the morning, concluding your unforgettable cruise experience.

Accommodation:

Staterooms and Suites: The cruise offers a range of accommodations from interior staterooms to luxurious suites with private balconies. Each room is designed for maximum comfort and aesthetic appeal.

Onboard Experience:

Dining: Enjoy a variety of dining options, including multi-cuisine restaurants offering Indian and international dishes. There are also specialty restaurants and cafes on board.

Entertainment:

The ship features a theater with live shows, a nightclub, and a casino. There are also numerous bars and lounges for relaxation and socializing.

Recreational Activities:

Facilities include a spa, gym, swimming pool, and a dedicated play area for children. There are also various games and workshops to participate in.

Additional Highlights:

Evening Parties: Make your evenings memorable with lively parties at the club. Dance to great music or unwind with a drink in hand.

Casino: Test your luck at the casino, offering a range of games for both novice and experienced players.

This cruise promises a perfect blend of luxury, adventure, and entertainment, making it an ideal choice for families, couples, and solo travellers looking to explore the Bay of Bengal's coastal treasures.

Day 1: Welcome Aboard

Begin your mesmerizing cruise adventure from Chennai, famously known as the city of dreams. Board the magnificent cruise and settle into your chosen accommodation, designed to provide comfort and panoramic ocean views.

Chennai, the cultural capital of South India, is a treasure trove of experiences. Don't miss exploring the iconic Marina Beach, the historic Fort St. George, and the divine St. Mary's Church. Discover the architectural marvel of Valluvar Kottam, built in honor of the esteemed Tamil poet Thiruvalluvar.

Return to the cruise for an evening of festivities. Enjoy vibrant music and exotic flavors at the dome party, complemented by delicious cuisines in the ship's bars and lounges. This marks the perfect start to your unforgettable cruise journey.

Day 2: Day at Sea

Embark on an exhilarating day filled with unlimited adventures as you sail through the open ocean. Delight in a plethora of global cuisines while cruising through the azure waters, offering a feast for your taste buds.

Rejuvenate your body and mind with a soothing spa session, where the mesmerizing ocean views enhance the experience. Try your luck at the casino, offering games from blackjack to roulette and everything in between, for an exciting day at sea.

Day 3: Arrive at Visakhapatnam

Arrive at Visakhapatnam, a city renowned for its stunning beaches and a blend of natural and man-made wonders. Known as Vizag, it is home to India's oldest shipyard.

Settle into your elegantly designed rooms, equipped with luxurious amenities to ensure maximum comfort. From your cabin, take in the serene ocean views and immerse yourself in the tranquility that surrounds you

Day 4: Day at the Sea

Enjoy your time on the cruise with your loved ones and make the most of this experience, filling you with sheer luxury.

Day 5: Arrive in Puducherry

Morning Arrival

Arrive in Puducherry, also known as the Paris of the South.

This unique destination on India's east coast offers the opportunity to scuba dive.

Shore Excursion:

Head out for a city tour to explore the stunning beauty of Puducherry.

Architectural Marvels and Arts :

Discover the architectural wonders and vibrant arts scene.

Enjoy the charming cafes scattered throughout the city.

Famous Attractions

Auroville: Visit the internationally renowned experimental township.

Aurobindo Ashram: Explore the spiritual community founded by Sri Aurobindo.

Paradise Beach: Relax on the pristine, sandy shores.

Botanical Garden: Stroll through the lush greenery and exotic plants.

Forest Wildlife Park: Experience the local wildlife in a natural setting.

Bharathi Park: Enjoy the serene atmosphere and beautiful landscapes.

Museums: Visit the various museums showcasing Puducherry's rich history and culture.

Day 6: Return to Chennai

◈ Pack your bags full of memories as you go back to the home port, only to visit again soon.

◈ Disembark at Chennai with unforgettable memories of cruising.

How to reach?
The cruise sails from Rajaji Salai Port, the famous port of Chennai. Arrive at the port of Chennai which is located at a distance of 25 km from Chennai's international as well as domestic airports, 3.8 km from the Chennai central railway station and around 4 km from the Egmore bus stand.

Note: The departure location of Cordelia Cruise might change depending on the weather conditions.

Accommodation: Interior room, accommodating up to 4 guests :

Duration: 6 Days / 5 Nights

Room Details:

Description: Comfortable, budget-friendly option with modern facilities and equipment for optimum privacy and great comfort

Room Size: 10.86 m^2

Package Price:

Standard Price: INR 66,789

Discounted Price: INR 56,054 per adult

Inclusions:

Stay: Interior room. Meals: All meals included at the Food Court & Starlight restaurant

Activities:

DJ and pool party

Balle Balle show

India through movies

Entertainment shows

Facilities:

Access to the swimming pool

Access to the fitness center

Access to all public areas and lounges

Child/Baby Policy:

Children below 2 years: Free of cost when accompanied by a paying adult

Children aged 2-12 years: Eligible for child prices

Extra Guest Policy:

Guests above 12 years: Considered adults and eligible for extra adult prices

Ocean View Room

Duration: 6 Days /5 Nights
Book your stay in the Ocean View Rooms which can accommodate up to 4 people. Spend some awesome moments in comfort by staying in this splendid ocean view room and grasping the views of the limitless sea. Enjoy the stay with lavishing interiors and modern amenities, that cater to a blend of comfort and relaxation.

~~INR 95,678~~
INR 71,801/Adult
Room Size
12.91 m^2
Inclusions

- Stay
    - Ocean View Room
- Meals
    - All meals are included at the Food Court & Starlight restaurant
- Activities
    - DJ and pool party
    - Balle Balle
    - India through movies
    - Entertainment shows
    - Access to the swimming pool
    - Access to our fitness center
    - Access to all public areas and lounges*

View Child/baby policy

- Children below 2 years can avail of the experience free of cost, accompanied by a paying adult.
- Children within the age group 2-12 years can avail themselves of the child prices.

Extra Guest Policy

- People above 12 years of age shall be considered adults and can avail of extra adult prices.

Mini Suite

Duration: 6 Nights D/5 Nights
Experience staying in the lavish balcony cabin with an attached balcony from where you can behold the soothing ocean blues. This stay option is embellished with a modernly designed interior and a double bed to accommodate up to 3 people with an ensuite bathroom that makes sure the guests enjoy their stay while on the cruise.

~~INR 1,45,678~~
INR 1,32,643/Adult
Room Size
18.11 m²
Inclusions

- Stay
  - Mini Suite
- Meals
  - All meals are included at the Food Court & Starlight restaurant
- Activities
  - DJ and pool party
  - Balle Balle
  - India through movies
  - Entertainment shows
  - Access to the swimming pool
  - Access to our fitness centre
  - Access to all public areas and lounges*

View Child/baby policy

- Children below 2 years can avail of the experience free of cost, accompanied by a paying adult.
- Children within the age group 2-12 years can avail themselves of the child prices.

Extra Guest Policy

- People above 12 years of age shall be considered adults and can avail of extra adult prices

Suite

Duration: 6D/5N
Book your stay in the luxurious suite on this Cordelia Cruise that can accommodate up to 3 guests. Relish optimum privacy and great convenience when you relax with the provision of modern facilities and equipment.

~~INR 2,79,999~~
INR 2,51,465/Adult
Room Size
28.14 m^2
Inclusions

- Stay
    - Suite
- Meals
    - All meals are included at the Food Court & Starlight restaurant
- Transfers
    - DJ and pool party
    - Balle Balle
    - India through movies
    - Entertainment shows
    - Access to the swimming pool
    - Access to our fitness center
    - Access to all public areas and lounges*

View Child/baby policy

- Children below 2 years can avail of the experience free of cost, accompanied by a paying adult.
- Children within the age group 2-12 years can avail themselves of the child prices.

Extra Guest Policy

- People above 12 years of age shall be considered adults and can avail of extra adult prices.

More Details about Cordelia Cruise | Chennai - Visakhapatnam - Puducherry - Chennai

Know Before You Go for Cordelia Cruise | Chennai - Visakhapatnam - Puducherry - Chennai

◇ It is important to abide by cruise policies and rules.

◇ Keep all the windows and doors of the room closed, when not inside or at night.

◇ It is advisable to consume alcoholic beverages on-board responsibly.

◇ Be attentive during the drill and instruction session conducted before the cruise sets sail. It will be important, in case of any emergencies.

◇ Advanced bookings are a better and hassle-free way of enjoying the cruise holiday as well as to ensure that you get the desired rooms.

◇ Keep the key card handy at all times along with all other documents, like package voucher, identification etc.

◇ In case of sea sickness, head to the on-board medical staff or any staff for help.

◇ It is mandatory to inform about any underlying or pre-existing medical conditions before the cruise.

◇ The guests mustn't befriend or interact with the performers and crew as it can result in escalated situations for both parties.

Section 4 : Cordelia Cruise | Chennai-Hambantota-Colombo-Kochi

◇ Escape from the bustling city life and take a joyful Chennai to Kochi journey on the luxurious Cordelia Cruise

◇ Spend a wonderful evening as you attend various amazing musical performances and magic shows at the Marquee theatre

◇ Visit the food court or various restaurants and treat your taste buds as you grab Indian or International delicacies prepared by professional chefs

◇ Have a comfortable stay in the well-maintained rooms which are designed with essential amenities to offer a relaxed feel

◇ Admire the panoramic views of the beautiful sunset and surroundings as you sit on the open deck area

Meeting Location: Island Grounds, Flag Staff Road, Port Trust Officers Quarters, Sathya Nagar, Chennai Port Trust, Chennai, Tamilnadu, 60009

Departure Dates (2024): 23 September

Duration: 6 Days 7 5 Nights

Note: The departure location of Cordelia Cruise might change depending on the weather conditions.

About the Cordelia Cruise:

Embark on an amazing journey from Chennai to Kochi via Hambantota & Colombo on the lavish Cordelia Cruise. Stay in well-maintained rooms which are furnished with essential amenities to provide comfort throughout the trip. Spend a memorable evening as you enjoy a range of musical shows and dance performances at the Marquee Theatre. With a range of amazing facilities like a spa, fitness center, outdoor swimming pool, theatre, food court, restaurants & bar, the cruise provides an unforgettable experience. Book the Cordelia Cruise, sit on the open deck area, and take in the outstanding views of the blue ocean.

Facilities:

◇ **Dining:** Enjoy delicious Indian and International cuisines in the Food court & various restaurants on the ship.

◇ **Casino:** Play various games at the casino with your friends and try your luck.

◇ **Bar:** Have a drink of the finest liquors including cocktails and spirits at various bars i.e. Chairman's Club, Connexions, & Pool Bar.

◇ **Fitness Center:** Visit the fully equipped fitness center at the cruise and complete your workout sessions during the journey.

◇ **Theatre:** Spend an amazing evening enjoying outstanding programs at the Marquee Theatre, including magical shows, musical performances, and more.

◇ **Spa:** Rejuvenate your body with a pampering treatment while enjoying the panoramic views of the sea at Spa & Salon.

◇ **Kid's Play Area: Visit the** playing area known as Cordelia Academy with your little ones where they will enjoy playing a range of fun-filled games.

◇ **Gaming Zone:** Get involved in some old-fashioned video games at the fantastic gaming zone, Challenger Video Arcade.

◇ **Reading Zone:** Spend time in the peaceful ambiance of the Reading Zone, take in the breathtaking views of the surroundings, and enjoy reading your favorite book.

About the Tour
Day 1: Welcome Aboard

- Start your journey from Chennai to Kochi as you board the luxurious Cordelia Cruise with your folks.
- Relax and unwind in your well-designed rooms or suites and have a comfortable feel.
- Explore the various unique zones available on the cruise, including the library, theatre & casino, and spend a wonderful evening.

- Sit on the open deck and marvel at the scenic ocean views while enjoying refreshing drinks.

Day 2: Day at Sea

- Enjoy a delicious breakfast, head towards the gym available on the cruise, and complete your workout sessions.
- Calm your senses and rejuvenate your body & mind as you take a soothing massage in the Spa & Salon.
- Bring your little ones to the Cordelia Academy where they will spend a fun-filled time participating in various games and group activities.
- Treat your taste buds to delicious Indian and international cuisine prepared by skilled chefs at the Food Court and various restaurants.
- Enjoy entertainment shows and performances at the theater or party at The Dome and spend an amazing evening with your folks.

Day 3: Arrive at Hambantota

- Reach Hambantota the next morning and explore this prominent town in Shi Lanka.
- Stroll through the streets and see famous attractions of the town like the Portuguese-built fort built in the 16th century.
- Roam around the city and admire the whitewashed villas and Dutch-style residences.
- Head back to the cruise in the evening and spend an amazing time playing games at the casino with your folks.

Day 4: Explore Colombo

- Reach Colombo, get off the cruise, and enjoy visiting the largest city & judicial capital of Shri Lanka.
- Explore some of the prominent landmarks like Galle Face Green, Viharamahadevi Park, Beira Lake & Colombo Racecourse, and know the city's ancient history.
- Stroll through the streets and satisfy your hunger with delicious local food in the city.
- Hop on the cruise again, satisfy your hunger with a scrumptious dinner, and enjoy your amazing journey to Kochi.

Day 5: Day at Sea

- Take part in exciting activities like rock climbing and safety drills and spend a fun-filled time on the cruise.
- Bring your little ones to Cordelia Academy where they will participate in a range of fun-packed games.
- Savor the finest culinary delights at the food court and multiple restaurants and satisfy your hunger.
- Have an unforgettable evening with your friends as you attend wonderful events and parties at The Dome.

Day 6: Arrive at Kochi

- Reach Kochi the next morning and end your amazing trip with lots of cheerful memories for the future.

How to Reach?

- **From City Center:** The meeting location is 4.4 km from Chennai city center. You can reach the location within 12 minutes by car/cab.
- **From Railway Station:** The meeting location is 5.9 km from Chennai Central. You can reach the location within 15 minutes from local or public transport.
- **From Airport:** The meeting location is 22.5 km from Chennai International Airport. You can reach the location within 56 minutes by car/cab.

Section 5 : Cordelia Cruise | Chennai Colombo Male Goa Mumbai

◇ Go on adventurous trip to Chennai, Colombo, Male, Goa, & Mumbai on luxurious Cordelia Cruise

◇ Be a part of evening party, entertainment shows, and try your luck at casinos

◇ Relax and have fun at the Pool Bar and Open Deck with stunning ocean views

◇ Visit historical monuments and beautiful beaches in Colombo

◇ Explore Maldives and go on shore excursion in Male

Check-In: 6:30 PM (Day 1)

Check-Out: 12:00 PM (Day 8)

About The Cruise:

Embark on an amazing trip to Chennai, Colombo, Male, Goa, and Mumbai on the magnificent Cordelia Cruise. Enjoy the 8-day holiday visiting these places with your loved ones or other companions onboard. Participate in adventurous activities, go for excursions, visit historical monuments, spend time on beautiful beaches and try your luck at casinos.

Along with the luxurious stay, you get access to Open Deck and Pool Bar where you can chill with the finest drinks and snacks. Have lip-smacking Pan-Asian cuisines, both vegetarian and non-vegetarian, prepared by professional chefs. Get mesmerized by stunning ocean views throughout and come back with cherishable memories.

About the Tour:
Day 1: Welcome Onboard

◈ Begin your cruise holiday as you board the Empress from Chennai.

◈ Check into your room and get ready for an entertaining, fun-filled, and adventurous holiday.

Day 2: Day at Sea

◈ Begin the day with a breakfast and experience the different fun and adventure activities we have onboard for you and your family.

◈ Enjoy some fun family time at the pool. Indulge in the gourmet cuisines and enjoy a cocktail at the Pool Bar.

◈ We have several activities and events planned for the evenings.

◈ Don't forget to try your luck at the casino.

Day 3: Explore Colombo
Arrival: 26,Sep 8:00 am
Depart: 26,Sep 9:00 pm

◇ Arrive in Colombo today morning and head for the shore excursions and activities as per your itinerary.

◇ The cosmopolitan city of Colombo is every traveler's haven.

◇ The city boasts of historical monuments and beautiful beaches.

◇ You will love the excursions and activities here.

◇ Don't forget to book your shore excursions.

◇ Make the best use of your time here before heading back to the cruise in the evening.

Day 4: Day at Sea

◇ Spend the day today enjoying the different activities and services onboard.

◇ Pamper yourself at the spa or the salon, or hit the gym before you load on the calories.

◇ Don't forget to take your kids to the Cordelia Academy, a fun and learning center for kids of all age groups.

◇ In the evening, enjoy the different entertainment shows and events, and party at The Dome.

Day 5: Explore Maldives
Arrival: 28,Sep 7:00 am
Depart: 28,Sep 5:30 pm

◇ Today morning, you will arrive at one of the world's most popular destinations, The Maldives.

◇ As per the schedule, head for your shore excursions and tours in Male.

◇ Spend the evening onboard the Empress cruising to your next destination.

Day 6: Day at Sea

◇ Spending the relaxing and enjoying our buffet spreads.

◈ From Pan-Asian cuisines to grills, we serve some of the best vegetarian and non-vegetarian options.

◈ Go for a swim, enjoy a couple of drinks at the Pool Bar and enjoy the stunning ocean views.

◈ If you haven't visited the casino yet, today evening is the best time.

Day 7: Experience Goa
Arrival: 30,Sep 1:00 pm
Depart: 30,Sep 7:00 pm

◈ Arrive in Goa today afternoon and as per the itinerary enjoy the activities and tours before cruising to your final destination, Mumbai.

Day 8: Arrive in Mumbai

◈ Arrive in Mumbai, today morning and disembark the cruise.

Selecting a seat on a cruise or a room is a highly personalized decision, influenced by various factors that cater to individual preferences and needs. Here are some considerations to help you make the best choice:

Location Preferences:

Proximity to Amenities: Some traveller's prefer rooms near elevators, dining areas, pools, or entertainment venues for convenience. This can minimize walking distances and make it easier to access the ship's main attractions.

Quiet Areas: For those seeking tranquility, selecting a room away from high-traffic areas such as elevators, staircases, and entertainment zones can provide a more peaceful experience.

Views and Balconies: Ocean-view or balcony rooms offer scenic views and a private outdoor space, ideal for those who enjoy fresh air and watching the sea. Interior rooms, while more budget-friendly, do not provide outside views but often offer a cozy and quiet environment.

Room Type:

Suites: Suites offer the most luxurious experience with ample space, upgraded amenities, and often come with exclusive services such as concierge or butler service.

Mini-Suites: A step down from full suites, these provide extra space and some enhanced features compared to standard rooms.

Ocean View Rooms: These rooms provide natural light and views of the sea, which can enhance the overall cruise experience.

Interior Rooms: These are the most economical choice, suitable for those who plan to spend most of their time exploring the ship and ports rather than in their room.

Budget:

Cost Considerations: Interior rooms are typically the most budget-friendly option, while ocean-view and balcony rooms come at a higher cost due to their added benefits. Suites are the most expensive but offer the most luxurious experience.

Value for Money: Consider how much time you plan to spend in your room versus participating in activities and excursions. If the room is primarily for sleeping, a less expensive option might be suitable.

Motion Sensitivity:

Stability and Motion: Passengers who are prone to seasickness might prefer rooms located mid-ship and on lower decks where there is less motion. These areas are generally more stable and experience less swaying compared to higher or more forward and aft locations.

PRIVACY AND SOCIAL Preferences:

Private vs. Social Areas: Balcony rooms and suites provide a private outdoor space, which can be appealing for those who enjoy privacy. On the other hand, interior and ocean-view rooms might be preferable for those who plan to socialize more and spend less time in their rooms.

Special Needs and Preferences:

Accessibility: Cruise lines offer accessible rooms for passengers with mobility issues, ensuring comfort and convenience.

Family-Friendly Options: Some rooms are designed with families in mind, offering extra beds, connecting rooms, or additional space for children.

Ultimately, the choice of a seat or room on a cruise is subjective and depends on personal priorities such as budget, comfort, convenience, and desired experience. Taking the time to consider these factors will help ensure a more enjoyable and satisfying cruise vacation.

Section 6 : Cordelia Cruise | Chennai-Kochi-Mumbai

Cordelia Cruise | Chennai-Kochi-Mumbai Highlights

⬦ Embark on an amazing journey from Chennai to Kochi & Mumbai through Cordelia Cruise and get an unforgettable experience

⬦ Stay comfortable during the trip as the rooms & suites are well-furnished with a range of essential amenities

⬦ Complete your training sessions in the fitness center on the cruise and stay active throughout the day

⬦ Satisfy your hunger with the finest culinary delights prepared by professional chefs at the food court & restaurants

⬦ Spend a memorable evening as you enjoy various entertainment shows and musical programs at the Marquee Theatre.

Meeting Location: Island Grounds, Flag Staff Road, Port Trust Officers Quarters, Sathya Nagar, Chennai Port Trust, Chennai, Tamilnadu, 60009

Departure Dates (2024): 25 April

Check-In/ Departure: 06:00 PM (Day 1)

Note: Please reach the meeting location one hour before departure.

Check-Out/ Arrival: 09:30 AM (Day 6)

About the Cordelia Cruise:

Escape from the bustling city life and immerse yourself in the scenic views of the ocean while enjoying an amazing trip from Chennai to Kochi & Mumbai. Feel luxurious as you spend a memorable vacation on the lavish Cordelia Cruise with your folks. The cruise includes premium accommodations, exotic entertainment, and one of the finest dining to provide an outstanding holiday experience. Stay comfortably in the well-designed rooms & suites and get a home-like feel. Indulge in a range of fun-filled activities on the cruise and make your vacations special.

Facilities:

◇ **Dining:** Tingle your taste buds with mouthwatering Indian and International cuisines in the Food court & various restaurants on the ship.

◇ **Casino:** Try your luck and spend a fun time with your folks while playing various games at the Casino.

◇ **Bar:** Take a sip of the finest liquors including cocktails and spirits at various bars i.e. Chairman's Club, Connexions, & Pool Bar.

◇ **Fitness Center:** Complete your workout sessions during this exciting journey as the fully equipped fitness center is available on the cruise.

◇ **Theatre:** Enjoy amazing programs including magical shows, musical performances, and more at the Marquee Theatre.

◇ **Spa:** Calm your senses and give a pampering treatment to yourself while enjoying the panoramic views of the sea at Spa & Salon.

◇ **Kid's Play Area:** Your little ones will love spending their day playing fun-filled games in the playing area, Cordelia Academy.

◇ **Gaming Zone:** Spend a fun-filled time with your friends as you play some old-fashioned video games at the amazing gaming zone, Challenger Video Arcade.

◈ **Reading Zone:** Enjoy reading your favorite book in the tranquil ambiance of the Reading Zone while admiring the breathtaking views of the surroundings.

About the Tour:
Day 1: Welcome Aboard

◈ Board the cruise from the meeting location and gear up for an unforgettable cruising experience on the luxurious Cordelia Cruise.

◈ Check into your well-designed rooms or suites and get a comfortable feel throughout the journey.

◈ Spend an amazing evening with your folks by either enjoying various activities or sitting on the upper deck.

Day 2: Day at Sea

◈ Enjoy a delicious breakfast on the cruise prepared by professional chefs and kick-start your day.

◈ Unwind yourself and calm your senses as you enjoy soothing therapies at Spa & Salon.

◈ Visit the Cordelia Academy with your children where they will indulge in a range of games & group activities.

◈ Feel adventurous while taking part in some amazing activities like rock climbing with your folks.

DAY 3: DAY AT SEA

◇ Spend another exciting day on the high seas with the luxurious comfort of the cruise.

◇ Head towards the fitness center and complete your workout sessions during the journey also.

◇ Visit the gaming zone i.e. Challenger Video Arcade and play classic video games with your friends.

◇ Satisfy your hunger with mouth-watering Indian & International delicacies in the food court and restaurants i.e. Starlight, Chopstix, and Chef's Table.

◇ Enjoy outstanding shows & musical performances in the Marquee Theatre and make your evening a memorable one.

DAY 4: EXPLORE KOCHI

⬥ Arrive in Kochi, one of the most culturally rich cities of Kerala, and gear up to explore its significant spots.

⬥ Go for shore excursions and admire the outstanding beauty of this delightful destination.

⬥ Take an amazing tour of this amazing city and know about the colorful identity of Kerala.

⬥ Head back to the cruise with lots of cherishable memories and spend the evening enjoying various entertainment shows.

Day 5: Day at Sea

⬥ Take a refreshing dip in the outdoor swimming pool and feel rejuvenated throughout the day.

◈ Sit on the open deck and immerse yourself in the breathtaking views of crystal blue waters.

◈ Enjoy refreshing drinks during a night party at the bar and make your evening a memorable one.

Day 6: Arrive in Mumbai

◈ Reach Mumbai and end your amazing trip here with lots of cheerful memories for the future.

How to Reach?

◈ **From City Center:** The meeting location is 3.4 km away from Chennai city center. You can reach the location within 10 minutes by car/cab.

◈ **From Railway Station:** The meeting location is 3.4 km away from M.G. Ramachandran Central Railway Station. You can reach the location within 10 minutes from local or public transport.

◈ **From Airport:** The meeting location is 24 km away from Chennai International Airport. You can reach the location within 58 minutes from local or public transport.

Section 7 : Cordelia Cruise Chennai- At Sea-Trincomalee-Jaffna-Chennai

Cordelia Cruise Chennai- At Sea-Trincomalee-Jaffna-Chennai Highlights

◇ Savour a feast of local cuisines served to you onboard & grab a glass of drink of your choice

◇ Visit several historic landmarks of Sri Lanka & know about the rich history of the region

◇ Explore the beautiful city of Trincomalee & Jaffna , two beautiful port towns in Sri Lanka, on your cruising journey with Cordelia

◇ Enjoy luxurious facilities onboard the Cordelia Cruise ship such as private balconies, fine dining & wellness facilities.

◇ Cordelia Cruise provides you with a range of fun options, from live music performances and comedy shows to movies & games.

Departure Dates(2024): 19 June, 17 July, 25 June, 14 August, 13 August, 20 August, 11 September

Note: The departure dates of the Cordelia Cruise might change depending on the weather conditions.

Check-in: 5:00 PM (Day 1)

Check-out: 01:00 PM (Day 4)

About The Cruise:

Embark for a luxurious cruising experience with Cordelia Cruises that lasts for 4 nights & 3 days, where you will be catered for lavish facilities onboard with a beautiful view of the sea. Go on a voyage of exploring the beautiful coastlines, serene waters & cultural heritage of the regions like Chennai, Trincomalee & Jaffna. Your cruising journey will begin from the port of Chennai, where you'll board the luxurious Cordelia ship.

The cruise is equipped with world-class amenities, fine dining & entertainment options to make your journey more memorable. Step on the deck of the cruise from where you can take in the amazing view while sailing across the serene waters of the Indian Ocean. Explore two beautiful port towns in Sri Lanka - Trincomalee and Jaffna, where you can gain cultural experiences & explore ancient temples, forts & also try the local cuisine. So, have the experience of going on a cruise journey to the beautiful cities of Sri Lanka on Cordelia Cruise with lush facilities & services and learn about the region's rich history & culture.

Facilities:

◇ **Luxurious Accommodation:** The ship offers luxurious cabins and suites with stunning ocean views, private balconies & modern amenities.

◇ **Fine Dining:** Enjoy multiple dining options available on board, including gourmet restaurants, cafes and bars serving a variety of cuisines from around the world.

◇ **Entertainment:** Your cruising journey will be loaded with a range of entertainment options, including live shows, music performances, movies, games & more.

◇ **Spa & Wellness:** Relax inside the spa or go for exercise in the fitness centre which helps you to refresh your mind & body.

◇ **Swimming Pools:** You can dive into multiple swimming pools, including a rooftop pool to get refreshed and enjoy the scenic view of the sea while sailing.

◇ **Kids' Zone:** Step inside the kid zone where you can play a range of activities & games to keep the young ones entertained.

About the Tour:
Day 1 - Board the Cruise:

◇ Your journey begins at Chennai Port, where you'll board the luxurious Cordelia Cruise ship.

◇ Settled down in your comfortable room then explore the ship's amenities, including restaurants, bars, and entertainment options.

◇ Enjoy a sumptuous lunch on board as you begin sailing towards At Sea.

Day 2 - At Sea:

◇ Your second day on the cruise will be dedicated to admiring the view of the surroundings as you see the beautiful & serene waters of the Indian Ocean.

◇ The cruise provides you with various options to relax as you can chill in the pool, take part in fun activities & games, or go to the spa.

◇ With an onboard bar, DJ, a small casino and a theatre, the ship offers a range of facilities to keep you entertained throughout the day.

Day 3 - Trincomalee:

◇ On the third day, the cruise will arrive at Trincomalee, a charming port town in Sri Lanka.

◇ Here, you can explore the natural beauty of the region, visit ancient temples and historic forts, and take a dip in the pristine waters of the beach.

◇ Taste different types of delicious Sri Lankan cuisine during your visit to the town.

Day 4 - Jaffna:

◇ On the fourth day, the cruise takes you to Jaffna, a city located in the northern part of Sri Lanka. Go out to know more about the rich cultural heritage of Jaffna by visiting ancient temples, museums & other historical sites.

◇ The city is also known for its delicious local cuisine, so make sure to try some of the specialities while you're here.

Day 5 - Chennai:

◇ As the cruise journey comes to an end head back to Chennai, where you'll disembark from the ship with lots of fun memories.

◇ But before that, you can enjoy one last day on board, relaxing & enjoying the ship's amenities.

◇ Don't forget to buy souvenirs while exploring the natural beauty & cultural heritage of the en-route region.

How To Reach?

◇ **From City Center:** The meeting location is 4.4 km from Chennai city centre. You can reach the location in 12 minutes by car/cab.

◇ **From Railway Station:** The meeting location is 5.9 km from Chennai Central. You can reach the location in 15 minutes by local or public transport.

◇ **From Airport:** The meeting location is 22.5 km from Chennai International Airport. You can reach the location in 56 minutes by car/cab.

Conclusion :

Embarking on a journey with Cordelia Cruises in India is more than just a vacation; it's an exploration of the country's stunning coastlines, rich cultural heritage, and unparalleled luxury. This conclusion aims to encapsulate the essence of traveling with Cordelia Cruises, highlighting the diverse experiences, exceptional services, and the profound impact such a journey can have on travellers. You can board any ship depending upon your requirement.

A Unique Blend of Luxury and Tradition

Cordelia Cruises offers a unique blend of modern luxury and traditional Indian hospitality, setting the stage for an unforgettable voyage. The cruise line's flagship, Empress of the Seas, epitomizes this blend with its elegant design, state-of-the-art amenities, and a dedicated crew committed to providing top-notch service. Travelers are treated to a luxurious experience that includes comfortable accommodations, gourmet dining options, and a plethora of entertainment activities.

From the moment you step on board, you are greeted with the warmth and hospitality that India is renowned for. The meticulously designed interiors, inspired by Indian culture and contemporary aesthetics, create a welcoming and relaxing atmosphere. This fusion of luxury and tradition ensures that every moment spent on the cruise is both comfortable and culturally enriching.

Exploring India's Coastal Gems

Cordelia Cruises offers itineraries that cover some of the most beautiful and culturally rich destinations along India's coastline. Whether it's the vibrant beaches of Goa, the historical charm of Chennai, or the tropical paradise of the Lakshadweep Islands, each destination offers unique experiences.

The shore excursions organized by Cordelia Cruises are thoughtfully curated to provide an in-depth exploration of each port of call. These excursions include guided tours, cultural performances, adventure activities, and opportunities to interact with local communities. This allows travelers to immerse themselves in the local culture and heritage, making their journey more meaningful and memorable.

A HUB OF ENTERTAINMENT and Activities

Onboard Cordelia Cruises, there is never a dull moment. The cruise offers a wide range of entertainment options that cater to all age groups and interests. From live music and dance performances to casinos and nightclubs, there is something for everyone. The ship also features multiple swimming pools, fitness centers, and spas, ensuring that guests have ample opportunities to relax and rejuvenate.

For families traveling with children, Cordelia Cruises provides a variety of kid-friendly activities and programs. These include play areas, educational workshops, and entertainment shows tailored to young audiences. This ensures that every member of the family has a fulfilling and enjoyable experience.

Culinary Delights

Food is a significant aspect of the cruising experience, and Cordelia Cruises excels in this domain. The cruise offers an array of dining options that include both Indian and international cuisines. The chefs onboard are adept at creating exquisite dishes that cater to diverse palates. Whether you prefer a formal dining experience or a casual meal, the culinary offerings on Cordelia Cruises are sure to satisfy your cravings.

Special themed dinners and culinary events are often organized, providing guests with a chance to indulge in unique gastronomic experiences. These events not only highlight regional specialties but also allow traveller's to savor the flavors of different cultures.

Comfort and Convenience

Choosing the right room on a cruise is crucial for comfort and enjoyment, and Cordelia Cruises provides a variety of accommodation options to suit different preferences and budgets. From luxurious suites with private balconies to cozy interior rooms, each option is designed to provide maximum comfort and convenience.

Travelers prone to motion sickness can opt for mid-ship cabins on lower decks, which offer greater stability. For those seeking privacy and stunning ocean views, balcony rooms and suites are ideal. The cruise also offers accessible rooms for guests with mobility issues, ensuring that everyone can enjoy their journey comfortably.

Environmental Responsibility

Cordelia Cruises is committed to sustainable and responsible tourism. The company employs various eco-friendly practices to minimize its environmental impact. These include waste management systems, energy-efficient technologies, and initiatives to reduce plastic usage. By choosing Cordelia Cruises, travellers can enjoy their vacation while contributing to the preservation of marine ecosystems and coastal environments.

Creating Lasting Memories

A journey with Cordelia Cruises is more than just a trip; it is an experience that creates lasting memories. The breathtaking views of the ocean, the cultural richness of the destinations, the luxurious accommodations, and the exceptional service all come together to make the voyage truly special. Whether you are traveling with family, friends, or as a couple, Cordelia Cruises offers an opportunity to create moments that you will cherish for a lifetime.

In conclusion, traveling with Cordelia Cruises in India is a unique and enriching experience that combines luxury, culture, and adventure. It allows travellers to explore the beauty of India's coastline, immerse themselves in local traditions, and enjoy world-class amenities and services. As you disembark from the cruise, you carry with you not just souvenirs, but a treasure trove of memories and experiences that will stay with you forever.

GT Holidays Private Limited

No.1, Gemini Parson Complex,
Kodambakkam High Road, Tirumurthy Nagar,
Nungambakkam, Chennai,
Tamil Nadu, India — 600006

+91 9940882200

mail@gtholidays.in

Thank
you!

Thank you for choosing my book! Your support means the world to me. As you embark on this journey through its pages, I sincerely hope it brings you joy, inspiration, and new perspectives.
Your feedback is incredibly valuable to me, so please consider sharing your thoughts and opinions by leaving your email ID for me to reach out. Your reviews help me grow as a writer and ensure that future readers discover the magic within these words.
Thank you for being a part of this adventure with me.

| Page